This is Fred.

1

Fred has a bed.

The bed is big and red.

Fred has things in his bed.

He has a bat, a rat, a cat,

and a flat hat in the bed.

He has Brett the pet

and a wet vet in the bed.

Bill, who is ill, is in the bed.

He can not skip up his hill.

Dot's pot, a rock, a sock,

a lock, and a clock are
in the bed.

A tub full of mud,

a truck, a pup,

and Fred

are in the big, red bed!